Bicycling
for *Fitness*

consultant:
Michael Klasmeier
Program Director
League of American Bicyclists
Washington, DC

LifeMatters
an imprint of Capstone Press
Mankato, Minnesota

by
Gus
Gedatus

LifeMatters Books are published by Capstone Press
PO Box 669 • 151 Good Counsel Drive • Mankato, Minnesota 56002
http://www.capstone-press.com

SPECIAL ADVISORY AND DISCLAIMER: The information within this book addresses fitness and sports
activities that carry significant safety risks, including the risk of serious personal injury. Because this book is
general in nature, we recommend that the reader seek qualified professional instruction and advice. We also
recommend the use of quality protective equipment when participating in fitness and sports activities. The
publisher, its consultants, and the author take no responsibility for the use of any of the materials or methods
described in this book nor for the products thereof.

Printed in the United States of America

Library of Congress Cataloging-in-Publication Data
Gedatus, Gustav Mark.
      Bicycling for fitness / by Gus Gedatus.
           p.   cm. — (Nutrition and fitness)
      Includes bibliographical references and index.
      ISBN 0-7368-0705-5
      1. Cycling—Juvenile literature. 2. Physical fitness—Juvenile literature. [1. Bicycles and bicycling.
      2. Physical fitness.] I. Title. II. Series.
      GV1043.5 .G43 2001
      613.7′11—dc21   00-037099
                                                    CIP

Summary: Explains the benefits of biking for fitness, what a workout includes, and how to design a
program. Also includes information on choosing the right bike and equipment, adjusting and maintainin
a bike, and riding laws and safety measures.

Staff Credits
Rebecca Aldridge, editor; Adam Lazar, designer and illustrator; Kim Danger, photo researcher

Photo Credits
Cover: Stock Market Photo/©David Stoecklein
©DigitalVision/Ronnie Eshel, 14
Index Stock Photos/©BSIP Agency, 13; ©Stewart Cohen, 17; ©Grantpix, 28; ©FotoKIA, 31; ©Tom Rickles, 37;
©Bob Winsett, 43; ©SW Production, 58
International Stock/©Tony Demin, 6, 9; ©Scott Barrow, 21 (left); ©Phyllis Picardi, 24; ©Bob Firth, 41
Photo Network/©Eric Rodriguez, 21 (right); ©Brooks Dodge, 59
Uniphoto/44, 50; ©Daemmrich, 22;©Bob Daemmrich, 55
Visuals Unlimited/©L. S. Stepanowicz, 49

Table of Contents

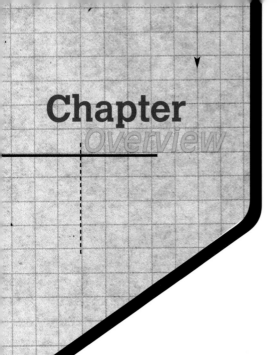

Chapter
Overview

- Physical fitness can help you remain healthy and enjoy work and play fully.

- Bicycling is one of the best forms of aerobic exercise. It improves cardiovascular fitness and muscular strength and endurance. It also can help balance the muscle and fat in your body makeup and give you extra energy.

- Bicycling is a great way to combine fun, relaxation, and fitness.

- You can make a fitness commitment to yourself.

Chapter 1

The Benefits of Bicycling

The Meaning of Fitness

What comes to mind when you hear the word *fitness*? Do you think of a weight lifter who has bulging arm and leg muscles? Maybe you picture billboards or TV commercials for exercise machines or health clubs. The term *fitness* can have different meanings for different people. Generally, physical fitness means that your heart, lungs, muscles, and blood vessels are in good working order. Often, the result of physical fitness is carefree, energetic work and play both now and in the future.

The Fitness Benefits From Bicycling

Bicycling is a great way to maintain good health and fitness. It's one of the best forms of aerobic exercise. This is exercise that uses large, steady body movements over a period of time. These body movements allow the muscles to get a continuous flow of fresh oxygen.

Cardiovascular Fitness

During aerobic exercise, your heart beats faster than normal. Such a workout gives you a higher level of cardiovascular fitness. That means it strengthens your heart and improves how your blood vessels work. Your heart pumps blood throughout your body more effectively. Your blood vessels carry oxygen to organs, muscles, and all other parts of your systems more effectively, too.

Bicycling helps to build lean and strong lower-body muscles.

As you exercise more and more, the muscles you use, including your heart, become better able to process oxygen. Exercise becomes easier. You can breathe more easily during exercise than you could before because your lungs work more effectively. You can ride for longer periods of time without getting tired out.

Because regular aerobic exercise makes the heart stronger, cycling can help reduce the risk of heart attack. Not many young people have to worry right now about heart problems. Wouldn't it be great, though, to have less worry about your heart when you're older?

Muscular Fitness

Have you ever walked home carrying heavy bags of groceries? Maybe you get tired and sore from the weight of your backpack filled with books. If your muscles are fit, such loads are easier to handle.

Muscular fitness includes both endurance and strength. How many times you can lift something and how long you can hold it is a matter of endurance. Your muscular strength determines how much weight you can lift. Many activities in your daily life, such as lifting grocery bags or carrying a backpack, test your muscular fitness.

Bicycling increases muscular strength and endurance, especially that of the lower body. Researchers say that it's as effective as walking or running for building strong, lean lower-body muscles. A bicycling program that includes riding up hills can strengthen the muscles of the back and shoulders. It may even strengthen these muscles more effectively than some weight-lifting programs.

Increased muscular strength, even in the lower part of your body, can help you to lift heavy objects. You can swing a baseball bat harder or jump higher to hit a volleyball. With greater muscular endurance, you are able to use muscles for a longer period without pain or fatigue.

Ronnie, Age 16

Ever since Ronnie was little, he's loved to eat. When he began kindergarten, he was one of the heavier kids in his class. Other kids liked phys. ed. class, but Ronnie didn't. It seemed like too much work.

First, Ronnie started bicycling to run errands for his parents. Biking seemed like less work than walking. After a while, Ronnie found that he liked to bike—just to bike. He started biking almost every day.

With his own simple biking pattern, Ronnie started losing weight. He still loves to eat, but he avoids junk food because it seems to slow him down. Many activities that used to seem like work to Ronnie seem fun now.

Calories Burned During Cycling

Bicycling speed in miles per hour (mph) and kilometers per hour (kph)	Calories burned per hour
10 mph or 16 kph	260
15 mph or 24 kph	465
20 mph or 32 kph	760
25 mph or 40 kph	1175
30 mph or 48 kph	1500

A Leaner Body

Think of your body mass as falling into two groups, your lean weight (muscle, bone, internal organs) and fat weight. For good health, you should maintain an appropriate balance of one to the other.

Food contains calories. These are the units of energy that fuel your body. Movement and activity require the use of calories. However, if your body can't use all the calories it takes in, it stores the extra calories as fat. Bicycling several times a week is a good way to burn calories and fat.

Cycling uses the largest muscles in your body. One is the quadriceps, the large four-part muscle at the front of the thighs. The other is the gluteus maximus in the buttocks. The buttocks are the fleshy part of the body where you sit. Bicycling works these muscles and increases your lean body weight.

Extra Energy

The exercise from cycling gives you more energy for other activities. As you develop more energy, you may actually enjoy everyday tasks such as cutting the grass or cleaning the apartment. As you become more fit, it may seem like you have more options for exercise and fun.

Bicycling: Fun and Freedom

Think of the possibilities. You can bike alone or with friends. You can ride four blocks, four kilometers, or four miles. You can bike in familiar places or explore new settings. You can relax in a fresh breeze under the sun while improving your fitness and clearing your mind.

You can enjoy the freedom of the outdoors while bicycling for fitness.

Unlike many other sports, bicycling offers great variety and few complications. You don't have to travel somewhere just to exercise at a gym. You don't have to reserve a court or pay a fee. You can combine your workout with errands.

Making a Commitment to Yourself

A bicycling fitness program allows you to challenge yourself. You can set your own personal goals and decide how hard to press yourself. Bicycling allows you to set up an exercise plan on your terms. You can do it for your own health, enjoyment, and sense of personal accomplishment. You don't have to compete against anyone but yourself.

Points to Consider

- In your opinion, how is biking unlike other sports?

- What types of aerobic exercise do you do regularly?

- What special challenges do you face whenever you make a commitment to yourself?

- What would be your main reasons for starting a cycling fitness program?

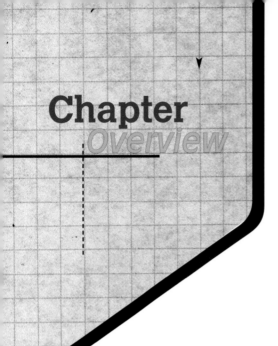

Chapter

Overview

- Determining your current fitness level before beginning an exercise program is a good idea.

- Repeating fitness tests and keeping track of your results can show you how your fitness is improving.

- Asking yourself some questions can help you decide how much bicycling to do in the beginning.

Chapter 2

Rate Your Fitness Before Making a Plan

If you've read this far, you're probably interested in improving your fitness through bicycling. Terrific! You may be excited and raring to go. However, before you begin, it helps to know your current fitness level. This information combined with the answers to some specific questions can be useful. These things can determine how rigorous, or challenging, your beginning cycling should be.

Fitness Tests

You can do some tests to determine how fit you are at the present time. Then you will have a better idea of how to approach your exercise program. The results of these tests can help you in setting goals.

Heart Rate

Heart rate, or pulse, is the number of times your heart beats in a minute. An ideal heart rate for a person at rest is between 60 and 90 beats per minute. In most cases, a person's resting heart rate decreases after a few months of regular exercise. This happens because the heart becomes more efficient. The chart on the next page shows how to determine your heart rate.

Some advanced bicyclists use heart rate monitors. When riding, they can keep track of their fitness program by measuring their heart rate. With a monitor, they can make sure they are pacing themselves correctly.

Resting Heart Rate Test

For this test, you need a watch or clock that displays seconds.

- Rest the ring, middle, and index finger of one hand lightly on the wrist of the opposite arm.

- Place these fingers directly between the base of the hand and the thumb. Then, feel for a beat.

- Count the beats for a full minute. The number of beats counted is your pulse. (You also can count your heartbeats for 15 seconds and multiply by 4.)

A person's aerobic fitness can be measured by his or her heart rate while working. A person's maximum heart rate can be calculated by subtracting that person's age from 220. During exercise, a person's target heart rate should be within 60 to 85 percent of the maximum. Subtract your age from 220, then multiply that number by .75 (75 percent). This is approximately the middle of your target heart rate range for working out.

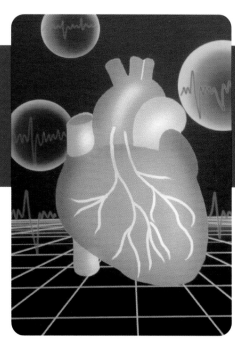

Your heart benefits from aerobic exercise such as bicycling.

Dennis, Age 18

Dennis wants to start a bicycling fitness program. However, before he works out, he needs to know the range for his target heart rate.

First, Dennis figures out his maximum heart rate. He subtracts 18 from 220 and gets 202. Then, he multiplies 202 by .60 to get the low end of his target heart rate range. For Dennis, this is 121 heartbeats per minute. Next, he multiplies 202 by .85 to figure out the high end of his target heart rate range. This rate is 171 beats per minute for Dennis.

Now Dennis knows that during a bicycling workout his heart rate should be between 121 and 171 beats per minute.

Aerobic Fitness

You can check your aerobic fitness with the following test. You will need a watch that displays seconds, a pad and pencil, and a treadmill or a running track marked at one mile or kilometer.

To do the aerobic fitness test, you'll need a stopwatch or a watch that displays seconds.

Aerobic Fitness Test

- Warm up slowly by walking for 5 to 10 minutes. Then, write down the exact time.

- Walk 1 mile or kilometer as fast as you can.

- Right before stopping, check your heart rate. Write it down.

- Write down the exact time you stop. Determine how long it took you to walk the mile or kilometer by subtracting the first time from the second.

- One minute after finishing the mile or kilometer, check your heart rate again. Write it down. This is called your recovery pulse. It should be much lower than your pulse taken right after finishing the mile or kilometer.

Keep the results in a safe place. Try the test again in a few weeks. As you cycle and improve your fitness, your time should get faster. Also, your first pulse taken should be lower. The difference between your first pulse and your recovery pulse should be greater, too.

Cycling works mostly the muscles of the legs, hips, and buttocks. When biking up hills, you also use upper-body muscles.

Did You Know?

Lower-Body Strength

You can check the strength of your lower-body muscles by trying the following test.

Lower-Body Strength Test

- On the floor, lie flat on your back with your arms next to your sides.

- Lift your legs upward, together, to a 45-degree angle. Then, bring them back down to the floor.

- Repeat the leg lifts until you're too tired to do any more.

- Record the number of times you were able to lift your legs.

How to Use Your Results

These tests can give you a general idea of your fitness level. A high score now means you can probably begin a harder cycling program than someone with a low score can.

Keep track of your results from these tests. Then repeat these tests as you work through your fitness program. Record these results as well. You may be amazed at the changes as your fitness improves.

Questions to Ask Yourself

Answering the questions in the following chart can help you decide how rigorously to begin your cycling.

What Kind of Program Am I Ready to Begin?

Read each sentence below. Then choose one of the words or phrases to the right that best describes you in relation to the sentence. On a separate piece of paper, write down the score for your answers. When you're finished, add up your score.

Score:	0	5	10
I have or have had heart or lung problems.	Not at all	Somewhat	A lot
I have or have had bone or muscle injuries.	Not at all	Somewhat	A lot
I feel out of breath.	Hardly ever	Sometimes	Often
I get muscle aches and cramps.	Hardly ever	Sometimes	Often
In the past, I have trained for cycling.	For a year	For a few months	Not at all
I get other strong aerobic workouts.	Daily	Weekly	Rarely
I am over my ideal weight by about . . .	0 to 9 lb* (0 to 4.1 kg**)	10 to 20 lb (4.5 to 9.1 kg)	More than 20 lb (9.1 kg)
I currently bike.	A lot	Sometimes	Not at all

pounds
** *kilograms*

Fitness tests and answers to some specific questions are useful. They can help you decide what kind of bicycling fitness program you're ready to start.

How to Use Your Results

If you scored 25 or less, you probably are ready to begin a rigorous bicycling fitness program. If you scored between 25 and 40, you may be ready to begin a gradually increasing fitness program. Those who scored between 40 and 80 should take biking slowly at first. People who have high scores should check with a doctor before beginning a bicycling program.

You will want to use the results of your fitness tests as well. For example, you may score 25 or less here. However, your fitness tests may show that you're not too fit. Then, you won't want to start out biking too aggressively.

Points to Consider

- What is your resting pulse rate? Why do you think it is this rate?

- Are fitness tests valuable? Why or why not?

- What questions do you think are important to ask before deciding on a beginning bicycling rate?

Chapter Overview

- Understanding how a bike works can help you in selecting and maintaining your bike.

- Three kinds of bikes are road, mountain, and hybrid bikes.

- It's important that you take some time and trial rides to find just the right bike.

- Make sure to get a bike with the proper frame fit for your body.

- There are many biking accessories. The most important is a biking helmet. A properly fitting helmet can protect you from many serious injuries in the event of an accident.

Chapter 3

The Right Bike and Equipment for You

How a Bike Works

Understanding a little bit about how a bike works can help you in buying, riding, and taking care of a bike.

The picture on the next page shows how the frame of a bicycle holds all the parts together. The fork joins the front wheel to the frame. Chain stays and seat stays connect the back wheel to the frame. Handlebars sit on a stem connected to the front of the frame. A seat post holds the seat, or saddle.

Pedals are connected to cranks on the frame. The brakes, also attached to the frame, are controlled by brake levers on the handlebars. The right hand controls the rear brakes. The left hand controls the front brakes. Front brakes are more effective than rear brakes.

As a rider's leg muscles move the pedals, a toothed gear near the crank moves the bicycle's chain in a big loop. The opposite end of this loop rests on one of the many toothed cogs connected to the rear wheel. The movement of the chain forces the back wheel to turn on its axle. As a rider shifts gears, the chain moves from one-sized cog to another. In the front, big chainrings mean big gears. In the rear, big chainrings mean small gears.

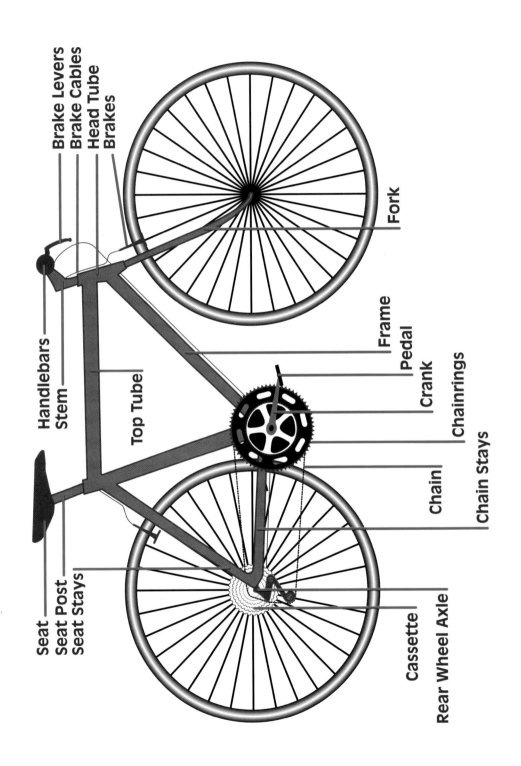

Brake Levers
Brake Cables
Head Tube
Brakes

Handlebars
Stem

Top Tube

Fork

Frame
Pedal
Crank
Chainrings

Chain
Chain Stays

Seat
Seat Post
Seat Stays

Cassette
Rear Wheel Axle

Bicycling for Fitness

Road bike tires are thinner than mountain bike tires. They also have less tread for traction than mountain bike tires do.

One revolution, or complete turn, of the pedal crank produces up to four revolutions of the wheel. The front wheel is used for steering and balancing. It is controlled by the rider and not moved by the chain.

Types of Bikes

Basically, three kinds of bikes are suitable for fitness cycling. Road bikes are lightweight and have skinny tires. They're excellent for riding on pavement. Their downward-curved, or drop, handlebars allow a variety of hand positions that can help avoid discomfort on long rides.

Mountain bikes are built for riding on dirt roads and trails. Their tires are wider than those of a road bike. Mountain bike tires also have deeper tread for traction, or gripping power, when riding on rough ground. Mountain bikes have flat or slightly upturned handlebars.

The third type of bike is the hybrid. This bike has wider tires than a road bike but narrower tires than a mountain bike. It's made for riding on pavement in a more comfortable upright position. That's because it doesn't have the downward-curved handlebars of a road bike.

Buying the Right Bike

You may take one look at a new or used bike and think it's just the bike for you. However, don't judge a bike by its looks. Take the bike and several others for a test ride before making a decision.

A helmet that fits properly is a necessary piece of biking equipment.

If possible, borrow bikes from friends, just to get the feel of different rides. If something minor bothers you about a bike, try another. A minor problem with the right fit could make future rides, especially long ones, pretty uncomfortable. After several test rides, you'll find the bike that feels right for you. If you have questions or doubts about buying a used bike, talk with an experienced cyclist who can give you some tips.

Allan, Age 17

When Allan was 14, he bought a used bike that didn't look perfect but rode decently. He learned to ride on that bike and made some repairs to it. Two years later he traded it for a better bike. On this bike, Allan became a skilled biker.

After Allan turned 17, he got a job and saved a lot of money fast. By this time, he knew exactly what he wanted in a new bike. When Allan went to the bike shop, he knew just what questions to ask. He knew how to tell if a bike felt right. After trying several models, he bought a great road bike that he plans to spend a lot of time riding.

If you plan on buying a bike from a store, you should be able to tell a salesperson what kind of riding you plan to do. Insist that the bikes you test ride be adjusted to your best riding position.

"I wear glasses. Once when I was riding, my glasses fell off and the frame broke. Now, I wouldn't think of riding without a neck cord on my glasses."—Damon, age 16

Teen Talk

The salesperson should offer to help you choose the proper frame size. This is important because unlike the saddle position, frame size cannot be adjusted. Here's one easy way to check the "frame fit." When you're in riding position, the handlebar and steering stem should block your view of the front wheel's hub, or center.

Another easy way to check frame fit is to stand over the center bar. The bar should be about 1 to 2 inches (2.5 to 5.1 centimeters) from your body for a road bike. It should be at least 2 to 3 inches (5.1 to 7.6 centimeters) from your body for a hybrid. For a mountain bike, the bar should be 3 to 4 inches (7.6 to 10.2 centimeters) or more from your body.

Accessories for Biking

People may tell you different things about what clothing and accessories are necessary for biking. Remember that it's okay to wear old tennis shoes and any shorts or shirt you want while biking. Special clothing made for cycling just makes riding more comfortable.

Helmets

The only extra equipment you must use is a helmet. Biking helmets help distribute and lessen the force of hitting your head if you have an accident. Studies have shown that helmets are important. When riders wear an approved helmet, 8 out of 10 serious head injuries are prevented.

Make sure that a helmet fits your head. A helmet that is loose can be almost as dangerous as wearing no helmet at all. You may borrow a helmet or be given a used one. In either case, you can buy inexpensive self-stick pads to make the helmet fit better.

Water bottles in cages and packs that attach to your bike keep needed items handy but out of the way.

Shoes

Shoes with nonslip soles are best for bicycling. Try one pair of your shoes, then another, and decide which seems best for cycling. You may want to buy cycling shoes. These shoes differ from typical athletic shoes. Good cycling shoes have stiffer soles that allow more of your power to move directly to the pedals. Cycling shoes often have cleats that attach to special bike pedals. If you're buying shoes with cleats, first find out whether both the shoes and the cleats fit your bike pedals.

No matter what kind of shoes you wear, make sure that they fit well. If they don't, you may develop blisters or other foot problems.

Riding Shorts and Pants

You'll be spending a lot of time in a seated position. Therefore, it's important to wear comfortable shorts or pants. Avoid shorts such as cut-off jeans. These usually have hard seams that may rub against your skin during a long ride.

Cycling shorts are padded for cushioning. You probably will find them more comfortable than most other shorts. Cycling shorts usually are made of the fabrics Lycra™ and nylon and have a high back. This provides a good fit while you lean forward on the saddle. These shorts are long enough to protect your thighs from rubbing on the saddle.

The skin on your buttocks and the inside of your thighs may become tender from rubbing against your shorts on long rides. Rubbing the inside of your shorts with vitamin A and D ointment before a ride may help. This ointment can soften rough fabrics, making them less likely to irritate your skin.

Did You Know?

Other Accessories

The other clothing you wear depends on the weather and how long you plan to ride. You might want to dress in layers. Then you can take off clothes as you become warmer. You might consider carrying a lightweight nylon windbreaker in case you get chilled.

You may want to attach a bike pack to the back of your saddle. Then you can carry extra clothing, snacks, and repair tools. Bike repair accessories are important, especially when taking a long ride. It's a good idea to carry a pump, just in case you have a flat tire. A frame-fit pump is small and clips easily under the top tube.

A water bottle is a necessity. Many water bottles have cages that attach to your bike frame. That way, you can carry water, yet it's out of your way.

You may need a bike lock for times when you must leave your bike unattended. Many bikers like to have a handlebar mirror, especially for riding near motorized traffic. If you plan on bicycling at night, front and rear lights are required by law in the United States.

Points to Consider

- Of the three kinds of bikes mentioned, which would you prefer? Why?

- What are some advantages to wearing a bike helmet?

- What are some bike accessories that you would most likely want? Why?

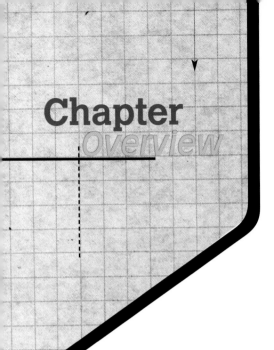

Chapter Overview

- You will want to adjust your bike saddle position and handlebar height to best fit your body.

- Making a last-minute maintenance check is a good idea before heading out on a ride.

- Your bike will perform best if it's kept clean and well oiled.

Chapter 4

Adjusting and Maintaining Your Bike

Adjusting Your Bike for Your Body

When you experiment with adjusting your bike, make one change at a time. That way, you can feel what effect the change has. And remember, it takes time to get used to a new position. Ride for a while in this new position before you decide whether a change is working.

When you make adjustments, use the correct size tool. If your wrench or screwdriver is too large, it can ruin the top of a screw or bolt.

Making your bike fit your body and your biking style may take a long time. You may have to make several adjustments to get the fit just right. If you still are confused about adjustments, you may want to get help from a local bike shop or a member of a cycling club.

It's important to adjust your bike saddle to fit your body. Correct saddle height helps you get the best use of your muscles while riding.

Saddle Height

The height of the saddle is the most important adjustment you can make. When the saddle is in the correct position, you make the best use of your muscles and you're more comfortable while cycling. You can find the right saddle height by following these four steps:

1. Have someone hold the bike from behind to help balance both you and the bike.

2. Sit squarely on the saddle and extend one leg until your heel comfortably touches the pedal. The crank arm should be in line with the seat tube.

3. If you cannot touch the pedal easily, the saddle is too high. If your leg reaches beyond the pedal, the saddle is too low.

4. Make adjustments to the saddle height if necessary. You might need to use a wrench to loosen the clamp on the saddle post.

"When you raise your bike saddle, make sure at least 2 inches of the saddle post stays in the seat tube. I raised mine too high one time and the saddle came off. Luckily, I had just stood up as I ended my ride. Otherwise, I might have hurt myself."—Annalise, age 17

Teen Talk

Front and Back Positioning of the Saddle

Once the saddle height is correct, you can adjust the front and back positioning of the saddle. Try a saddle position that allows your knees to be comfortable when both pedals are at an even height.

Making large adjustments to the front and back position of the saddle may affect height. You may have to check seat height again. Tilting the saddle forward is similar to moving the entire saddle down. Tilting the saddle back raises the distance to the pedals.

Handlebar Height

Experienced bikers usually want their handlebars to be about 1½ inches (3.8 centimeters) below the saddle height for road bikes. Those who ride mountain bikes usually want the handlebars at an even height with the saddle. While learning, you may prefer a different height. As you gain experience, you may want to consider a different height to flatten your back and improve your aerodynamics. This is your ability to move quickly and easily through the air around you. Be careful not to move handlebars past the maximum height marked on the stem.

Fast Fact

If you use a stationary bike in addition to your standard bike, try to keep the seat and handlebar heights the same on both. This makes it easier for you to go from using one to the other.

Last-Minute Checks

Before heading out for a ride, it's a good idea to do a few checks. Fixing things is easier to do at home than out on the road. Your tires should have plenty of air. Tires on road bikes usually require 100 pounds per square inch (psi). Mountain bike tires generally need 40 to 50 psi. You can check the air in your tires using a pressure gauge.

Good brakes are essential. Squeeze the brake cables to make sure there is enough tension. By releasing the straddle wire, or short brake cable, you can check the brake pads for wear. Brake pads with ⅛ inch (.32 centimeters) of material or less need to be replaced.

Make sure the bike chain moves freely. Chain links may become a little stiff. Check the wheels to make sure they are well fastened. It might be a good idea, before you take off, to check the saddle position. The height or angle may have shifted slightly since your last ride.

Taking Care of Your Bike

Try to keep your bike clean and well lubricated, or well lubed. To keep a bike lubricated, you use a special liquid that keeps bike parts from getting too dry. When applying chain lube, try to aim the lube directly where it's needed. Using too much chain lube or letting it collect or run can attract dirt to sensitive places. This can affect your bike chain especially. Dirt combined with too much oil in the chain can make it wear out faster. Wipe the chain with a rag to remove the excess lubricant.

Keeping your bike well lubricated means your bike will ride its best.

You may ride through mud puddles sometimes. When you do, it's a good idea to clean the dirt off your bike when you get home. Don't use a hose. The pressure from a hose might force water to the inside of moving parts. Instead, use a pail of warm water and a brush. If you use a lot of water on the chain, add some chain lube when you're finished cleaning. If you have any questions about taking care of your bike, talk with people at a local bike store for advice.

Points to Consider

- Why is it important to properly adjust your bike before starting out?

- What checks may you want to make before taking off on a ride?

- What are some important tasks in taking care of your bicycle?

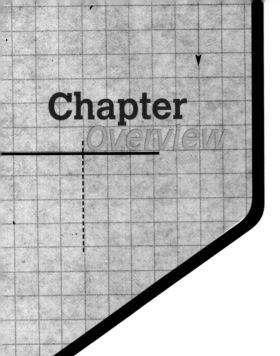

Chapter
Overview

- Learning to ride comfortably takes time and patience.

- Smooth, relaxed pedaling is a key to efficient riding.

- Many aches and pains from biking can be avoided. You can make changes to improve your riding style.

Chapter 5

Riding Basics

If you are just learning to ride, the first rule is to be patient. When biking, you have many things to think about, such as balancing, pedaling, and shifting. You even have to concentrate to drink from a water bottle while moving! Give yourself time. Practice on paths where there are no cars and few other bikes or pedestrians. People walking are pedestrians.

Riding the Right Way

The secret to good cycling is smooth, relaxed pedaling using the ball of your foot, not the heel. As you develop a comfortable pedaling pattern, your ride will flow. You'll end up putting less stress on your knee joints and riding more efficiently.

How fast a bicyclist pedals is expressed in revolutions per minute (rpm). A good rate for a beginning cyclist is 70 rpm. You can figure out the rate of your pedaling. For 15 seconds while riding, count each time your right leg pushes down the pedal. Multiply this number by four. That is your rpm.

After a few weeks at 70 rpm, you can increase your pedaling rate. A good goal is to pedal 85 to 100 rpm consistently during a ride. It may take up to six months to reach this goal.

Spinning out may happen while you ride. This means your feet can't keep up with the pedals. If this occurs, you need to shift to a higher gear.

Highest gear:
Hardest to pedal

Lowest gear:
Easiest to pedal

Learning to shift gears can help you maintain a high rpm while riding. The ground you ride on and the wind affect how much shifting you need to do. Hilly areas require low gears. Mechanically, being in the lowest gear means the small chainring is looped to the biggest rear cog. Low gears allow you to pedal in more rpms. This makes it easiest to pedal a bike. Riding on flat land means you will use high gears. In your bike's highest gear, the big chainring is looped to the smallest rear cog. This makes a bike the hardest to pedal.

Eventually, shifting patterns become automatic—almost like breathing. You learn to shift to keep pedaling at a constant rate.

Steering a bicycle is not just about turning the handlebars. A practiced biker slightly shifts his or her weight and leans just a little to make turns more easily.

Coretta, Age 14

Coretta was thrilled to get a new bike. The only thing that she wasn't too sure about was shifting gears. She got a book from the library that had a section on how gears work. Shifting gears seemed pretty complicated. She decided to ask Phil, the man at the bike store.

"All you really need to know as a beginner is this," Phil told her. "The more teeth you have on the chain ring in the front, the harder the bike will be to pedal. The more teeth on the cogs in the back, the easier it will be. For uphill, you'll want to use a small chainring in front and a big cog in back. For downhill, it's just the opposite." The answer was simple enough. Coretta was glad she asked.

Aches and Pains

Most of the aches and pains that some cyclists get can be avoided. The most important way to stay pain-free is to work gradually into your cycling program. Don't hop on your bike and ride 10 miles the first day. Start out with a short distance and then gradually add distance on your next rides. Warm up, stretch, and cool down with each workout. These activities are discussed in Chapter 7. It's possible that you might get some aches and pains that you can't explain. If so, the chart on the next page may help.

Avoiding Pain During a Ride

Area of Pain	Possible Ways to Correct It
Shoulders ache	Lean with less weight on the handlebars. This may require adjusting the saddle.
Neck is stiff	You may be holding the handlebars too low (perhaps on the curved underside of a road bike). This forces you to hold your neck at an angle to your back. Try holding the handlebars higher.
Lower back aches	Try lowering the saddle so you don't extend your leg fully every time you pedal.
Knees ache	Your saddle may be too high, which puts a lot of pressure on your knees. Another possibility is you may need to ride in a lower gear. If your knees are cold, you may want to get knee pads.
Hands or wrists ache; fingers are numb	You may need to put less weight on your hands by leaning a little less. Maybe you are holding the handlebars too tightly. Sometimes, varying your hand positions can help. You may want to add padded handlebar grips or wrap tape around the handlebars. For some people, padded cycling gloves help.
Buttocks feel sore or numb	You may need to adjust your saddle so it's more even or so it slants slightly toward the front. You may try wearing padded cycling shorts. If these steps don't work, try another saddle that is a better fit for you.
Leg muscles are tight	Do more stretching before your ride and take breaks to stretch your legs during a ride.
Legs cramp	You may be dehydrating, so drink more water while you ride. Perhaps you are riding too long too quickly. You may not be warming up and stretching enough.
Feet are sore or numb	Consider wearing shoes that have thicker soles and are less flexible. Another possibility is your shoes may be too tight.

Bicycling for Fitness

Stopping to stretch during a ride can help keep your muscles from getting too sore.

If you start tensing up during a ride or feel some muscle getting sore, you can help your body. Get off your bike and do some slow, gentle stretches of the muscle or muscles that are bothering you.

Points to Consider

- What is the difference between high and low gears?

- Why do you think it can take up to six months to pedal consistently at 85 to 100 rpm?

- What regular activities would you do to prevent some of the aches and pains that can come from cycling?

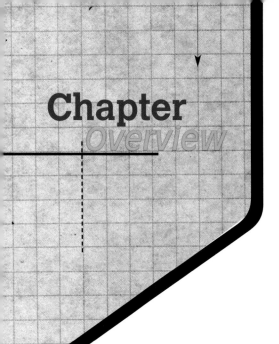

Chapter
Overview

- Whether traveling in the city, in the country, or on biking trails, choose your routes carefully.

- Bicyclists should obey the same traffic laws as cars, trucks, and buses.

- Safety practices can become habits that will help protect you from harm.

- Sometimes biking injuries are more serious than we realize. You might want to get help from someone.

Chapter 6

Out on the Open Road

Biking in the Country or City

You may live in an area that has miles of great, paved bike paths. These may be a good choice for your biking routes. Generally, these paths have smooth, predictable surfaces. Also, in most cases, bike paths are away from the dangers of motorized traffic. What you may find, though, is a lot of bike traffic on these paths. Other riders may move much faster or slower than you do, which can complicate your ride. You might check out the paths at different times of the day when there may be less traffic. When you do ride on paths, always announce to other path users your intention to pass or stop.

If you are planning to ride on country roads, choose them carefully. The best, safest roads have wide, paved shoulders. The wide shoulders of some country roads have a gravel surface. Unless you have a mountain bike with softer, fatter tires, you could be in for a pretty bumpy ride.

In the city, it's best to travel roads and streets that have few traffic lights and stop signs. It's also a good idea to stick to roads that don't have much traffic. Doing this allows you to continue without a lot of stops and starts, so you can keep up your exercise pace. Streets with fewer cars mean spending less energy trying to remain safe, too.

"I like to ride on cloudy days because I don't get so hot. But let me tell you something, I never thought about getting sunburned. On one of those cloudy days, my face got really burned. Now, I always put sunscreen on my face. I also rub some on my arms and legs when I wear short-sleeve shirts and shorts."—Jenna, age 15

Wherever you are bicycling, the following ideas can make your trip more carefree:

- Carry a small amount of cash in case you have a problem and need to use a telephone.

- If you're riding in one direction, and then back, begin against the wind. That way, when you're tired and on your way home, the wind will be with you, making pedaling easier.

- No matter how familiar you are with a certain area, it's a good idea to carry a map, just in case you get lost.

Marie, Age 16

Marie was about 10 miles from home when it started to rain. The rain was light, and Marie was determined to keep going. Then the wind started. Pedaling became difficult, but Marie wasn't going to stop. Then Marie saw lightning. She was glad she had remembered to put a couple quarters in her bike pack.

She stopped at a gas station a few blocks ahead and called her dad. When her dad arrived, he was great. He put her bike in the trunk and told Marie she did the right thing.

To signal a left turn, hold your left arm straight out.

Laws to Obey

In most parts of North America, bicycles are considered vehicles that must move according to traffic laws. By obeying traffic laws, you are much less likely to be injured. The following are traffic laws all bicyclists should obey:

- Come to a complete stop at stop signs.

- Stop at red lights. Move only when the light turns green.

- Ride with traffic, not against it. Stay to the right of the lane, unless glass or storm grates force you into the road.

- Don't ride the wrong way down one-way streets.

- Use an arm signal when planning to turn or come to a stop. Put your right arm straight out for a right turn and your left arm straight out for a left turn. To show that you are planning to stop, put your left arm out. It should be bent at the elbow, with your hand pointing straight down.

- When making a right turn, turn from the right shoulder of the road. When making a left turn, wait for a break in traffic. Signal and then proceed left to get to the correct lane before turning.

Many people ride stationary bikes at home or in gyms. These cycles provide most of the same fitness benefits as other bicycles. The "ride" may not be as interesting, but the rider doesn't have to worry about dealing with heavy motorized traffic. Also, the rider can watch TV, read, or listen to music at the same time.

- Yield to merging traffic.

- Yield the right of way to pedestrians.

- Have lights on the front and back of your bike when riding after dark.

- Never use a bicycle if under the influence of alcohol or other drugs.

Safety Concerns

Often when cyclists are on a relaxing ride, they forget about daily cares. Sometimes they even daydream as the breeze blows past them. However, wise cyclists keep attention focused on their surroundings. This is the key to preventing accidents. Your surroundings include cars, other bicycles, pedestrians, dogs, and even the ground beneath you.

Falls

About half of all bike accidents are falls. These may occur when a cyclist takes a turn too quickly. Sometimes they happen when firm pavement suddenly changes to loose gravel at a corner. They can happen if there is a nasty rut in the road that a cyclist doesn't see.

Collisions With Vehicles and Other Bicycles

Collisions with cars and other motorized vehicles cause 10 to 20 out of every 100 accidents. The numbers are similar for collisions with other bicycles. These accidents don't have to happen. You can practice defensive bicycle riding. This means you are on the lookout for others who are moving in both the same and different directions as yourself.

Call out for help if you have a bike accident and think you have broken a bone.

What to Do If You Have an Accident

You most likely will not have a serious cycling accident. However, accidents can happen. In the event of a minor injury, only you can decide whether to continue. You may be wise to reschedule your ride for another day. Pressing on when you've been hurt may make an injury worse. Also, an injury could be more serious than you realize. You may want to call a relative or friend for help.

If you take a fall on a busy path or near motorized traffic, try to move yourself and your bike out of the way. You don't want to be a part of a second accident with another vehicle. Call out to people passing by. Other cyclists, skaters, and runners are likely to help you. They would want you to do the same for them.

If you're injured and believe you have broken bones, wait and ask for someone to call for help. It's a good idea to bike with others if you are going to be traveling on remote paths. Then, if you are injured, there will be someone else who can help.

You need to have bike lights to ride safely at night.

Safety Practices

Here are a few practices that can help keep your biking experiences positive ones:

- Keep your bike in top working condition.

- Become skilled in riding on quiet routes before riding in busy places.

- When riding near motorized traffic, try to choose roads with wide, paved shoulders. Ride in a safe, defensive manner.

- Ride in a straight line. If you weave back and forth, other moving traffic won't know what to expect.

- Be careful when approaching an alley or a blind intersection. You may have the right of way, but someone coming from the side may not see you.

- Look over your shoulder occasionally. This may take practice and a slight weight shift to keep your ride smooth.

- When you are about to pass another biker, skater, or runner, announce your presence by saying something like, "Bike on your left."

- When you brake, your weight is pushed forward. If you have to stop suddenly, use your arms to push your weight backward.

Advice From Teens

- If you're riding alongside parked cars, keep a close watch on those cars. Someone may be getting ready to move back out onto the road. Someone else might be getting ready to open the driver's side door. This could become a sudden obstacle. A good rule of thumb is to ride 4 feet (1.2 meters) away from parked cars. That way, you can avoid getting hit by someone opening a car door.

- Don't ride directly behind moving cars. They may come to a sudden stop faster than you can stop your bike.

- If you're riding at night, wear bright-colored clothing. You might want to put reflective tape on the sides of your bike.

- Always wear an approved cycling helmet.

Points to Consider

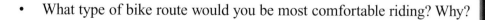

- What type of bike route would you be most comfortable riding? Why?

- What are some things to consider when planning your bike route?

- How would you deal with a serious fall on a bicycle route that you might be likely to take?

- In your opinion, what are the most important safety practices while bicycling? Why?

Chapter Overview

- Warming up prepares the body for a workout.

- Stretching can prevent your muscles from getting sore after a ride.

- A workout should include 20 to 30 minutes of cycling that keeps your heart in its target heart rate range.

- Three kinds of riding include long, steady distances, intervals, and sprints.

- Cooling down allows your body to return gradually to a resting level.

Chapter 7

The Parts of a Bicycling Workout

Warming Up

Many people prefer just to get to the fun of biking, without warming up. However, a warm-up is important. It helps you maintain energy and perform better and makes injury less likely. A warm-up consists of easy physical activities that prepare the body for a more strenuous workout. It may include activities such as jumping jacks, sit-ups, or slowly running in place. A warm-up should last about 5 to 10 minutes.

Judd, Age 15

Judd was late for the workout ride he had planned with two friends. When they arrived at his house, both of them had been biking for some time. Judd didn't take the time to warm up.

After only a few miles, Judd felt like he was going to collapse. He didn't want his friends to tease him about not keeping up, so he pushed himself. The pain turned to numbness as the ride came to an end.

The next day Judd was miserable. His hips, legs, and ankles were throbbing with pain. Next time, no matter what, Judd was going to take the time to warm up before riding.

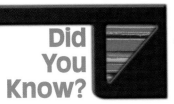

Sports medicine experts recommend biking over jogging because it puts less strain on muscles and joints.

Imagine someone wakes you up in the middle of the night and starts asking you lots of tough questions. You might say, "Wait a minute. Let me wake up before I have to think." You need a little time. Likewise, your body does not work its best when it must go directly from rest to intense activity. You can make this change gradually, warming the muscles as you go. Warm muscles contract more quickly. This means that oxygen is better delivered to those muscles. Then, by the time you're out on the open road and pedaling fast, your muscles are ready.

One effective warm-up consists of riding your bicycle at a slow, gentle pace for 5 to 10 minutes. Some people prefer to jog slowly as a warm-up. Whatever you do, don't push yourself too hard. Also, while warming up, try to move your arms as well as your legs.

Stretching

After warming up comes stretching, which makes muscles more elastic. Muscles that are warmed up and then stretched are more efficient and can produce more strength.

Stretching movements should be relaxed and easy. Most stretches should last 20 to 30 seconds. As you slowly stretch each part of your body, imagine blood rushing to this particular body part. Imagine the area becoming more flexible.

Try to stretch as many muscles as possible. This includes your calves, hips, lower back, and hamstrings. Your hamstrings are the bands of tissue at the rear of the hollow behind the knees. It's also good to stretch the Achilles tendon. This is the large band of tough tissue that runs from the back of the heel bone to the calf muscle. Another muscle to stretch is the quadriceps.

Stretching your hamstrings before a ride prepares these muscles for your bicycling workout.

Of these muscles, stretching your calves and hamstrings is especially important. However, those muscles that tire first when you ride are the most important. If you have trouble with neck stiffness, stretch your neck. Following are examples of stretches for the calves and hamstrings. You may want to ask a physical education teacher, a coach, or a doctor for some good stretches for the other muscles mentioned.

Hamstring Stretch

- Sit with your legs wide apart. Extend one leg. Bend the opposite knee, sliding your heel toward your crotch.

- Keep your back straight. Lean forward slowly and try to grasp the toes of the extended leg. Don't bounce.

- Then switch which leg is extended and which one is bent. Repeat.

Calf Stretch

- Stand facing a wall or other vertical surface from 1 foot or 30 centimeters away. Extend one leg behind you. Keep both feet flat on the floor with toes pointed forward. Keep your rear knee straight.

- Move your hips forward while keeping your lower back flat.

- Lean into the wall until you feel tension in the calf of your extended leg.

- Hold for 10 seconds, then stretch the other leg. Repeat.

During sprints,
you ride for speed.

It's best to stretch for at least five to eight minutes before a workout. Once all your muscles feel warm and flexible, you're ready to begin your cycling workout.

Working Out

The workout itself should last at least 20 to 30 minutes. During this time, your heart should be working in its target heart rate range. For good aerobic fitness, workouts should take place three to five days a week.

Types of Riding

You can include three different types of riding in a bicycling workout. The first kind is riding long, steady distances. The second kind of riding is called interval riding. The third type of riding is called sprinting.

Long, Steady Distances

Riding long, steady distances provides a low-intensity workout. Such riding is good for burning fat and increasing the strength of your heart and lower-body muscles.

Intervals

Interval riding is a high-intensity workout in which you switch work phases, or intervals, with rest phases. The work phases are short periods of anaerobic activity. During this activity, the body can't deliver oxygen fast enough to burn fat. The rest phases are longer phases of aerobic activity. Interval riding helps to improve power and speed.

Some people have one leg that is stronger than the other. Trainers often recommend that these people use a stationary bike to pedal with the weaker leg while resting the stronger leg.

Fast Fact

Sprints

When sprint riding, you ride for speed. You might use time trials, in which you race yourself against the clock. Sprint riding increases muscular strength and power. It also improves your reaction time.

Cooling Down

Cooling down after bicycling is just as important as warming up before you start. A cool-down is like a warm-up in reverse. A warm-up helps your cardiovascular system and muscles get going. A cool-down helps them slowly return to a resting level. That includes helping your blood get back to a normal flow. When you're cycling, blood collects in the wide-open vessels in your legs. A cool-down helps blood return to your heart and relocate throughout your body.

A good cool-down after cycling can be as simple as five minutes of walking or easy cycling. After your cool-down, do slow stretches, particularly of the muscles in your legs, lower back, and buttocks. Stretch any other muscles that are sore. Then, rest awhile to give your blood a chance to circulate normally again. You're less likely to feel light-headed if you do this.

Points to Consider

- What kind of warm-up would you do before cycling?

- Why are warming up and cooling down important to a workout?

- What muscles would you stretch before riding? Why?

- What type of riding do you think you would enjoy most? Explain.

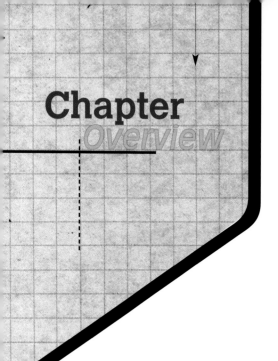

Chapter
Overview

- Create your own fitness program; don't try to follow someone else's.

- Charting or journaling your progress helps monitor your improvement and may point out any need for change.

- A healthy diet is vital for an effective bicycling fitness program.

- Cross-training can help you to achieve overall fitness.

Chapter 8

Setting Up a Fitness Program

To set up a bicycling fitness program, the first thing you need is a goal. What do you want to accomplish? What degree of fitness do you want to develop within the first six months? the first year? the first two years?

The Right Exercise Plan for You

A bicycling fitness book may outline a specific plan. However, you can't expect to follow someone else's plan. You have to set one that's appropriate for you. The following is a list of things for you to think about as you plan your fitness program:

- What are my physical strengths and weaknesses?

- What specific fitness goals do I have?

- How long can I ride without stopping? What speed can I maintain without tiring too quickly?

- What kind of riding environment is available to me?

"My friends and I wanted to keep bicycling fun and interesting. So, we started our own biking club."—Salma, age 14

- How can my program be altered if a change, such as bad weather or illness, occurs?

- If the program turns out to be too tough for me right now, what would my alternate plan be? How would that plan be different?

- What can I do to keep my program fun and interesting?

Tanya and Deb, Age 15

Tanya and Deb both started bicycling during the first week of June. At the end of the month, they went riding together. Deb had a hard time keeping up.

"I feel like there's something wrong with me," said Deb. "For most of our ride, you were pedaling much faster than I was. And now you're not even tired."

"That's true," said Tanya. "But don't forget that I jump on the trampoline or play ball with my little brothers a lot."

After that, Deb spent much of her free time riding. By fall, Tanya and Deb were riding at almost the same rate.

All right. You're excited about your fitness program. That's good. However, remember to start out slowly and build your workout gradually. You're more likely to succeed by slowly working into a program than by taking on too much at once.

Derek chose to start his bicycling program by riding on flat roads. He gradually worked up to tackling hills.

A Sample Plan

Following is 15-year-old Derek's bicycling fitness program to improve his muscle tone and increase his cardiovascular fitness. Derek set up his program for a steady ride, mostly in low gears. He tried to keep his pedaling at about an average of 90 rpm. He wrote down the time in which he hoped to complete each ride.

Derek's First Six Workouts

Ride 1   5 miles, 20 minutes, flat roads

Ride 2   6 miles, 25 minutes, flat roads

Ride 3   8 miles, 30 minutes, flat roads

Ride 4   5 miles, 20 minutes, series of low hills

Ride 5   6 miles, 25 minutes, hills

Ride 6   7.5 miles, 30 minutes, hills

Derek got through his first six rides in three weeks. He did some additional short, easy rides during those three weeks, as well as some swimming and basketball. He had no trouble with his goals on the first two rides. He was over his goal on Ride 3 by about one minute. He repeated Ride 3 just because he wanted to. The second time, he came in at his goal of 30 minutes. On Ride 4, his first day on hills, he was only one and a half minutes over. On Ride 5, he was seven minutes over. He wasn't quite ready for the steeper hills. He repeated Ride 5 a couple times. On Ride 6, he was under by about one minute.

Many bicyclists participate in century rides. They bike 100 miles in one day.

For his next set of workouts, Derek increased the mileage and the time. He spent more and more time climbing hills. This meant that he spent more time shifting and working some of his upper-body muscles.

Keeping Track of Your Progress

An important part of making goals effective is keeping track of your path toward your goals. You may decide a specific goal is not realistic. You may decide to make a change, perhaps in your choice of routes, distances, or pacing.

You may want to create a chart that you can use each month to track your progress as a bicyclist. You can use the chart on the next page or design your own.

Some bicyclists keep a training journal. In this journal, cyclists record their daily workout regimen, or plan. They note how far they traveled and in what time. Some people also keep track of their daily pulse rate before, during, and after their workout. Some people write down details of cross-training activities.

Your Diet and Bicycling

Eating a healthy, balanced meal about two hours before bicycling is important for maintaining energy. Foods such as pasta, bread, potatoes, and rice are high in carbohydrates, the most important fuel for physical activity. For rides longer than 45 minutes, your body may need a recharge. So, you may want to pack fruits such as grapes, raisins, or bananas, as well as fruit bars or energy snacks. Remember that energy bars and drinks are meant as snacks, not as replacements for healthy meals.

Bicycling Chart

Date	Speed	Location	Time	Pulse	Notes

Lifting weights is one example of cross-training that helps build upper-body strength.

While on rides longer than 45 minutes, drink plenty of water. You will be able to continue doing your best if you regularly replace the water your body loses. Take sips of water before you feel thirsty. It's a good idea to drink water during and after even a short ride.

If you usually eat lots of fruits and vegetables, vitamin supplements probably aren't necessary. However, if you don't eat many fruits and vegetables, you may want to take a multivitamin. It should contain vitamins A, C, and E. Try to eat something healthy within two hours after your ride, too. This helps replenish your system. If you don't do this, you may end up feeling tired the next day.

Cross-Training

When you become a regular cyclist, you develop fitness associated with cycling. The muscles of your lower body become stronger. As you continue training, you may feel there's no limit to the distance or speed you can achieve. However, to develop total fitness, you need to cross-train so that other areas of your body get a workout, too.

You may want to try some swimming or rowing. You may want to work out with weights occasionally. Perhaps you can play tennis, handball, or racquetball to help build strength in your arms, back, and chest.

On days when you don't bike, you may want to do some chin-ups, push-ups, or sit-ups. You may get a fitness boost from playing basketball. A variety of workouts helps keep you from getting bored and gives you physical flexibility. It sets a pattern for a lifetime of fitness and good health.

Your program is likely to succeed if you enjoy yourself!

Your Program

For your workout program, mix some hard rides with some easy ones. Give yourself at least one day off each week. Often, it's best to do a low-intensity ride after your highest-intensity ride of the week. Pay attention to your body and don't overdo it.

At the end of the year, it's important to take a break of up to one month. This helps you to avoid getting bored and to explore other areas of interest. After your break, start again with some low-intensity rides each week and cross-training. Get back into your program and enjoy yourself!

Points to Consider

- In your opinion, what is the most important thing to remember in setting up a bicycling workout program?

- What are some reasons for charting or journaling your workout progress?

- How would your bicycle fitness program differ from the one set up by Derek? Why?

- What cross-training activities would you add to your bicycling program?

NOTE At publication, all resources listed here were accurate and appropriate to the topics covered in this book. Addresses and phone numbers may change. When visiting Internet sites and links, use good judgment. Remember, never give personal information over the Internet.

Internet Sites

About.com—Bicycling
http://bicycling.about.com/sports/bicycling
Includes links divided by sections such as beginning cycling, nutrition, exercise/training, maintenance/repair, and more

CyberCycle
http://library.thinkquest.org/10333
Contains repair information, live chat, a biking game, and more bicycling discussions in a site students developed

CycleCanada
www.cyclecanada.com
Provides links to cycling clubs and events in Canada

Do It Sports
www.doitsports.com/cycling
Contains many articles of interest to cyclists

The WWW Bicycle Lane
www.bikelane.com
Provides a long list of bicycling-related links including organizations, teams, and clubs, as well as others

Useful Addresses

Canadian Cycling Association
2197 Riverside Drive, Suite 702
Ottawa, ON K1H 7X3
CANADA
www.canadian-cycling.com

International Mountain Bicycling Association
1121 Broadway, Suite 203
PO Box 7578
Boulder, CO 80306
1-888-442-4622
www.imba.com

League of American Bicyclists
1612 K Street Northwest, Suite 401
Washington, DC 20006-2082
www.bikeleague.org

For Further Reading

Baker, Arnie, MD. *The Essential Cyclist.* New York: Lyons Press, 1998.

Langley, Jim. *Bicycling Magazine's Complete Guide to Bicycle Maintenance and Repair for Road and Mountain Bikes: Over 1,000 Tips, Tricks, and Techniques to Maximize Performance, Minimize Repairs, and Save Money.* Emmaus, PA: Rodale Press, 1999.

Pavelka, Ed, ed. *Bicycling Magazine's Cycling for Health and Fitness: Use Your Machine to Get Strong, Lose Weight, and Feel Great.* Emmaus, PA: Rodale Press, 2000.

St. John, Allen. *Bicycling for Dummies.* Foster City, CA: IDG Books, 1999.

Glossary

aerobic (air-OH-bik)—requiring oxygen, air; energetic exercise that strengthens the heart and improves the cardiovascular system.

aerodynamic (air-oh-dye-NAM-ik)—designed to move through the air easily and quickly

cardiovascular (kar-dee-oh-VASS-kyuh-lur)—relating to the heart and blood vessels

cog (KOG)—one of the teeth on the front chainring or rear of a bike that turns machinery; people often call the chainring and sprockets of a bike cogs because they're toothed.

cross-train (KRAWSS-TRANE)—to do different types of exercise to work toward overall fitness

dehydration (dee-hye-DRAY-shuhn)—lack of enough water in the body

fitness (FIT-ness)—when a person's body is in good physical shape; a person's heart, lungs, muscles, and blood vessels are in good working order.

frame (FRAYM)—the main part of a bike that holds the other bike parts together

gear (GIHR)—a set of wheels with teeth that fit together and change the movement of a machine

pedestrian (puh-DESS-tree-uhn)—someone who travels on foot

regimen (REJ-uh-muhn)—a system or pattern for doing something

revolution (rev-uh-LOO-shuhn)—a complete turn of a body on its axis

saddle (SAD-uhl)—the seat of a bicycle

shifting (SHIFT-ing)—changing gears while bicycling

Index

accessories, 23–25

accidents, 23, 42–43

aches, 16, 35–36

Achilles tendon, 48

aerobic exercise, 5–6, 16, 50
    and your fitness level, 11, 12, 13–14

alleys, 44

anaerobic activity, 50

arm signals, 41

bicycling
    benefits of, 5–9
    intervals, 50
    long, steady distances, 50
    riding basics, 33–37
    sprints, 51

bike chain, 19, 30

bike pack, 25, 40, 56

bike shops, 7, 22–23, 27, 31, 35

bikes, 19–25. *See also* accessories;
    hybrid bikes; mountain bikes;
    road bikes
    adjusting, 27–30
    buying, 21–23
    caring for, 30–31
    how they work, 19–21
    types of, 21

biking clubs, 7, 54

brakes and braking, 19, 30, 44

buttocks, 8, 15, 25, 36, 51

calves, 48–49

cardiovascular fitness, 5–6, 55

checks, last-minute, 30

clothing, 25, 45. *See also* cycling
    shorts; helmets; shoes

collisions, 42

cooling down, 35, 51

cross-training, 56, 58

cycling clubs. *See* biking clubs

cycling shorts, 24, 36

defensive bicycle riding, 42, 44

diet, 7, 56, 58

dirt, 30–31

endurance, 6–7

energy, 5, 8, 47, 56

falls, 42, 43

fat burning, 7, 50

fat weight, 8

feet, 24, 33, 34, 36

fitness, 5
    aerobic fitness, 12, 13–14
    heart rate, 11–13
    lower-body strength, 15
    questions to ask yourself, 15–17
    rating your, 11–17
    tests, 11–15, 16–17

fitness programs, 9, 15–17, 53–59
    sample plan, 55–56
    tracking your progress, 56, 57

frame, 19, 23

gears. *See* shifting gears

goals, 9, 33, 53, 55, 56

hamstrings, 48–49

handlebars, 19, 21, 29, 36

hands, 36

heart, 5, 6, 50
    rate, 11–13, 14, 56, 57

helmets, 23, 45

Index